# Peter's Friend
# JESUS

By
Ruth Williams Lang

Peter's Friend Jesus
Trilogy Christian Publishers
A Wholly Owned Subsidiary of Trinity Broadcasting Network
2442 Michelle Drive
Tustin, CA 92780
Copyright © 2022 by Ruth Williams Lang
Scripture quotations marked amp are taken from the Amplified® Bible (AMP), Copyright © 2015 by The Lockman Foundation. Used by permission. www.Lockman.org.
Scripture quotations marked GNT are taken from the Good News Translation® (Today's English Version, Second Edition). Copyright © 1982 American Bible Society. All rights reserved.
Scripture quotations marked MSG are taken from THE MESSAGE, copyright (c) 1993, 2002, 2018 by Eugene H. Peterson. Used by permission of NavPress. All rights reserved. Represented by Tyndale House Publishers, Inc.
Scripture quotations marked NLT are taken from the Holy Bible, New Living Translation, copyright © 1996, 2004, 2015 by Tyndale House Foundation. Used by permission of Tyndale House Publishers, Inc., Carol Stream, Illinois 60188. All rights reserved.
Scripture quotations marked NKJV are taken from the New King James Version®. Copyright © 1982 by Thomas Nelson. Used by permission. All rights reserved.
Scripture quotations marked KJV are taken from the King James Version of the Bible. Public domain.
All rights reserved, including the right to reproduce this book or portions thereof in any form whatsoever.
For information, address Trilogy Christian Publishing
Rights Department, 2442 Michelle Drive, Tustin, Ca 92780.
Trilogy Christian Publishing/ TBN and colophon are trademarks of Trinity Broadcasting Network.
For information about special discounts for bulk purchases, please contact Trilogy Christian Publishing.
Manufactured in the United States of America
Trilogy Disclaimer: The views and content expressed in this book are those of the author and may not necessarily reflect the views and doctrine of Trilogy Christian Publishing or the Trinity Broadcasting Network.
10 9 8 7 6 5 4 3 2 1
Library of Congress Cataloging-in-Publication Data is available.
ISBN#: 978-1-68556-557-2
ISBN#: 978-1-68556-558-9 (ebook)

# Table of Contents

    DEDICATION . . . . . . . . . . . . . . . . . . . . . . . . . . 5

    ACKNOWLEDGMENTS . . . . . . . . . . . . . . . . . 7

1. FAITH TO WALK ON THE WATER . . . . . . . . 9
   *Walking on the water with the Lord*

2. THAT SINKING FEELING. . . . . . . . . . . . . . .15
   *Are you really saved?*
   *Jesus in the depths of our sadness*

3. PETER, "WHAT DID YOU ASK?" . . . . . . . . ..27
   *A fresh perspective*
   *Traveling buddy*
   *Getting permission*
   *Abraham's obedience*

4. TAKE COURAGE . . . . . . . . . . . . . . . . . . . . . .43
   *Fight fear with faith*

5. THE WALK BACK TO THE BOAT . . . . . . . . .55
   *Speaking to Him and about Him*
   *Peter's strength*

6. THE POWER OF PRAYER . . . . . . . . . . . . . . . 71
   *Speak the Words of power*

7. A FINAL THOUGHT . . . . . . . . . . . . . . . . . .. .81
   *Make a plan*

8. A COVID ADDENDUM . . . . . . . . . . . . . . . . .85

# Dedication

This book is dedicated to my dear forever friend Christine.

One of the brave, smart, lovely, and fun women I know.

# Acknowledgements

I first want to thank my perfect heavenly Father, His Son, my Jesus, and my precious Holy Spirit. Without your approval, love, insight, and Word, this would be an unfinished request or an empty attempt at a task that was fulfilling and daunting. I am forever devoted in love to You.

I'd like to thank my husband for encouraging me to write and being one of my staunchest supporters. Your belief in me and what I can do seems only shadowed by your faith in God, which is so great! I love you.

I need to thank my children, who are the adorable inspiration to some of my stories, the immeasurable pride and joy of my heart, and four of the most amazing humans I have the pleasure of knowing and loving.

Thank you, Dad of blessed memory, Mom, Denice, Maria, Barb and Maggie. Nowhere on earth is there a rowdier or more devoted cheering section, thanks for your support. I love you more!

And thanks, Christine, even before you read my first book, you believed I had it in me to write this one, my faithful friend. Love you.

A special thank you to Mark Mingle, Account Executive at Trilogy Publishing who believed in my book and patiently and happily answered so very many questions; Karin Brisbin, my Project Manager who kept me at a steady pace with much reassurance and optimism; Kara Franklin my Editor and encourager while shaping up this piece with expertise; and to JP Staggs my Graphic Designer who with precision and grace put a cover together that speaks so much about the content of my book. I'm delighted to have had the privilege to work with such a gifted group.

# 1

# Faith to Walk on the Water

Tremulous groans floated above the sea from the shocked veteran fishermen. The view they had, connected them to the now, by mere fact that all of them saw this "apparition" as they declared it. As He drew near, with the stride so familiar, He urges them not to fear. The first man recovered from astonishment, pushed the others further into shock by asking if he might try this adventurous walk. He waited, eager to escape the usual and step onto the new and previously unheard-of act of walking on water! Jesus said, "Come."

Leaping over the side of the boat, Peter excitedly ventured toward his astonishing Teacher. No one knows precisely the timing, but excitement gave way to panic as reality of waves churning under his feet overruled the exhilaration, he began the feat with. As faith gave way to fear, Peter sank, yelled a distinct S.O.S. and waited for the dependable arm of his Instructor to get him back on the level. "Why doubt, Peter?" questioned the Master. The companions completed their walk back to the boat, perhaps relishing the unquenchable delight of doing this.

As they scaled the side of the boat, tranquility arrested the robust waves and wind.

**Matthew 14:22-33**
**(author's paraphrase)**

Faith to walk on the water. That's what Peter had, or maybe just a bit of momentary crazy zeal! I suppose he had experienced enough power at Jesus' side that he thought that running out to Him was in the realm of possibilities too! He did, however, use a bit of restraint when he first asked Jesus, "Lord, if it is You, command me to come to You on the water." Peter was the first to acknowledge fully who He was, "You are the Christ, the Son of the living God," but he still first asked permission (Matthew 16:16, AMP). In that acknowledging, he knew that Jesus was obviously able to walk out on the waves, but was he, himself? At least for a few amazing steps! Perhaps, as he proved a few historic moments later, that even in the beckoning and excitement, the waves and winds of adversity and challenge can get close enough to cause fear, doubt, or other counter-faith reactions, such as sinking, in Peter's case at this moment. "So, Peter got out of the boat and walked on the water, and he came toward Jesus. But when he perceived and felt the strong wind, and as he began to sink, he cried out, Lord, save me (from death)!" (Matthew 14:29-30, AMPC).

The Lord gives us encouragement and unction and, in some cases, a Prophetic Word about moving into our calling, a new place to live, a new job or venture to try, the next step after a big challenge or trauma, or any other move that He needs us to take to begin work on the next thing He has in store for our lives. He says to us, like He said to Peter, "Come!" and hopefully, with the same exuberance with which Peter splashed down on top of the deep, we run to the new thing He has planned and purposed at that particular time. Many are as adventurous as Peter, going where others wouldn't without a clear direction or Word or desire and idea inside. Others do need the extra encouragement and repeated prompting by the Holy Spirit, friends, family, etc. to get going on it. Either way, obedience and movement are the way to blessing and fulfillment.

We, like Peter, step out into never experienced arenas and begin a new thing with a step of courage and hope that we'll accomplish that which we set out to do. We embrace the hard as well as simple tasks while we work. We talk to others about the "new thing" in our lives and get excited, many times bringing them along the journey to provide for them updates and receive from them encouragement and inspiration.

Then it happens, we encounter a bump in the road, twist in our step, get tripped and fall, are overwhelmed by timetables and deadlines, or any other challenge that makes us sink! Sometimes, we're caught off guard and end off a cliff of adversity with a long, arduous mountain to climb to get us back to where we left off. Know what I mean? Smooth sailing on a high of excitement and anticipation of a desired result or achievement, and then something or someone takes the wind out of your sails or, even worse, capsizes the boat! Sometimes there are signs of the impending danger. Sometimes it's more like a sudden, unexpected tragedy that pounces on you and knocks you off your feet and brings you to your knees.

It happened to Peter, and it happens to us. And then when we pray appropriately, Jesus shows up as He so expertly does and lifts us up, out, away, and on our path to His purpose. And I don't know about you, but after those experiences, I follow Him closer, hold on tighter, and travel more wisely in His company. "May Christ through your faith (actually) dwell (settle down, abide, make His permanent home) in your hearts! May you be rooted deep in love and founded securely on love" (Ephesians 3:17 AMPC).

Let's let Jesus and Peter teach us the way to go for it! Get the okay, step out in faith, and if we lose our way or footing, get faith back in our sight and walk the rest of the way with Him.

# 2

# That Sinking Feeling

That sinking feeling, Peter had it literally! We do have the experience as well. In times of trial, trouble, and suffering, we inhabit a totally different atmosphere with a totally different attitude and set of emotions and behavior. At least at the onset of it. I know that many of exceeding levels of maturity can remain completely levelheaded and calm under the greatest of challenges and trials, life experiences teach this. But some of us, in the most traumatic moments, will still give in to the release of whatever comes forth from the bowels of our being to be seen and heard by whomever is around at that moment.

- Perhaps a yell while watching a tough (bad) call at a ball game.
- A resounding "Yeah!" when our child or that of someone else we know scores an amazing point in a game or competition.

- A tremendous sigh/groan at the news of the passing of a loved one extremely close to us.

- Gasping in shock at the breaking news story that captivates and astonishes the world; be it natural disaster, pandemic, etc.

- An angry yell with a scowl to match when that last nerve has been jumped on.

- Disbelief and horror at the terror at work in our world, all too often.

The list goes on and on of the variety of things that can rock our world and senses in a blink of an eye, as well as our reactions and responses to them. I believe, when we react like Peter, shouting out to the Lord for help, peace, salvation, or saving us out of whatever other fix we're in is about the very wisest action we can take!

During a very harrowing experience driving to work, I had an extreme example of a similar response happen. I was traveling to work from my home. I was a teacher at a massage school and was, let's say as my husband does, "flowing with the traffic at a good speed in the fast lane." Suddenly (and it really was!) grey/black smoke started to pour out of every opening of the interior of my vehicle. Immediately, I could no longer see my hands on the steering wheel, let alone the road in front of me. To say I was shocked and concerned would have been an understatement! However, I believe I was guided into prayer because all that came out of my mouth was, "Jesus, I can't see where I'm going! You have to drive!"

Within seconds after speaking this pleading phrase, my car died, smoothly stopped completely. I didn't think again, but immediately opened my door to get out, not knowing if my car was actually on fire; or if I had made it to the side of the road, the center, or all the way onto the shoulder at the other side of the freeway. Well, to my tremendous relief, my vehicle had been parked before dying on the left shoulder of the highway, safe and out of harm's way. Thank You, Jesus! Needless perhaps to say, all flowing traffic was clear across away from me, and who could blame them!

As I stepped back watching my car literally going up in smoke, but not on fire, a precious man came running towards me and urging me to "please back away from the vehicle" as he wielded a pint-sized fire extinguisher. Well, I don't know how much that extinguisher might have done, but his rescue was like a breath of fresh air and put a smile on my face and serious joy in my heart! He also informed me that he had already called 911, so in a matter of minutes, I was surrounded by all types of heroes and somewhat relieved although still a bit shaky. After giving many thanks to all the gentlemen who helped me, I was towed and set on track again.

So, my heater core went, whatever that means (my husband and mechanics know). No damage to the inside of my car except one slightly melted vent. Amazing! Thanks to God, no accident and no one else in danger, including me. Jesus does and will save us in so many ways.

"Calling to the crowd to join His disciples, He said, 'Anyone who intends to come with me has to let Me lead. You're not in the driver's seat; I am'" (Mark 8:34-35, MSG).

"For it is by free grace (God's unmerited favor) that you are saved (delivered from judgement and made partakers of Christ's salvation) through (your) faith. And this (salvation) is not of yourselves (of your own doing, it came not through your own striving,) but it is the gift of God" (Ephesians 2:8, AMPC).

Yes, this scripture speaks primarily of the salvation that comes when we dedicate our lives to the Lord, the redeeming salvation, setting us free from our sins and allowing us the benefits of the promises He gave. However, as in Peter's and my case, He is faithful to us beyond the point of spiritual salvation and saves us in a myriad of ways.

THAT SINKING FEELING

# ARE YOU REALLY SAVED?

When speaking to my dad once about his salvation and accepting Jesus as his Savior, I asked if he was saved and also if my mom was, you know, really saved. Had he done the salvation prayer and taken the Lord into his heart, and he said yes, but that was only the beginning of his Christian walk. What he was getting at, was that the relationship was a commitment not only to the Lord in word, but as it becomes evidenced in our lives. When we adhere to the Word of God and make it come alive in our lives, put it inside our souls so it becomes us or we become it, the transformation takes place. We also become acquainted with the promises God gave us. For instance, "I will not fail you or forsake you" (AMPC) or as the Message Bible puts it, "I won't give up on you; I won't leave you" (Joshua 1:5).

Peter certainly found that out as he courageously embraced the astounding invitation to walk on the water, as I did when I left the driving to Him as I blindly continued down the road in faith! The other more significant facet of Joshua 1:5 is not only the realization of God's awesome capacity in the face of our own human weakness and inadequacy but the fact that He's so close to us that He sees the need and delivers the answer to that need in His perfect timing. Peter and I at these moments preferred God's quick involvement. Sometimes, the answer comes a bit slower or not as we might want it, but in the long run, it is the best thing to happen to us. I was reminded by Him the other day that, "Father knows best."

## JESUS IN THE DEPTHS OF OUR SADNESS

The saddest day of my life by far (I said and realized it later) was the day and ensuing days after my own father went home to be with the Lord. The day before it happened, I spoke to him after my husband and I had just gotten ultrasounds done for our unborn twins, confirming all was well and at least our son was obviously a boy, but our daughter was modestly hidden behind him and still a mystery. We shared the good news with him and were all pleased to be anticipating the birth of cute babies Judah and Mariah in that (insisted upon) order. The last words we spoke to each other were, "I love you, Daddy" and his "I love you, too, Dear."

The next day, I was standing in our friend's kitchen and chatting with her and my husband. We were temporarily staying with them as our house was being constructed and past the originally promised finish date. We praise God for them and another friend family as well as my mother-

## THAT SINKING FEELING

in-law and sister-in-law who all let us come invade their tender territories and spend some very special times with them.

My phone rang, and it was my sister who did not sound quite like herself and asked if she could please speak to Claude. I thought nothing of it, you see because his birthday had just passed, and I thought she and her family were calling to sing happy birthday to him as we often do for each other. He got on the line and then, a few minutes later, went upstairs to talk. My curiosity was peaked, but I let them have their moment—she had just turned the same age a couple months prior. Claude came downstairs a few moments later and asked Mendy if she could watch our two toddlers along with her own. She agreed and we went upstairs to talk.

The next few hours are somewhat a blur, but the very next few moments remain fixed clearly in my mind. My husband sat us down on our bed and said, "Honey, I don't know how to tell you this but to just say it. Something terrible has happened." I said, "Okay." He then said it in the gentlest way he could, but it was a blow that hit me directly in the heart. "Dad is gone." I was confused and said, "What?" He said, "Dad died." "What... whose dad?" And he said, "Your—our dad."

Silence...

Many more words of denial and confusion came from me until finally I looked at him and said quietly but insistently, "Get...me...home."

In my time alone with the Lord, I was concerned about my father's whereabouts. I knew we had the conversation about salvation for him and my mother, but I needed reassurance. After voicing my concerns and waiting, I was assured by that still small voice that Dad was with Him, and it was time to say good-bye. Then the tears, soft sobs, and the heaving chest. It was at this point that I really needed Jesus to pick me up and walk with me through the next days, weeks, and months to sort in my mind and being, the part of going on without that person you shared such a precious relationship with. He helped me know that the greater the love, the greater the grief, and that depth of grief was therefore a blessing to be grateful for. I am so grateful for the relationship I had with my father and now so joyous of the knowledge of where he is. Also working out my own salvation with all I have every day so I can behold the beauty of the holiness of our Lord and spend time with Dad again someday.

In all the going through the ins and outs of heaviness, sadness, tears while remembering the good times, and tears of settling into the new family we became without him there, I know that my reaching out to God as well as His own to me were the most essential parts of my recovery process. Walks to enjoy the gorgeous sunsets; watching my precious babies sleep, play, eat, and wrap a healthy layer of adorable joy around my heart and head; dates with my sweetheart when he told me how much I, our children, and our life together meant to him; and helping others in the same situation of loss whenever I could, helped me walk to the next chapter of my life.

My prayer was to be healed and able to move on swiftly, but the answer was a progressive one of endurance and participation in all the moments of sorrow; questions of his surprising and early demise; the acceptance of it; and concern for my mother, sisters, aunts and uncles, and his friends. Many other elements, some cloaked in misery and others in peaceful resolve, all had to be sorted out in my mind, emotions, and memories as much time passed. The presence of faithful friends and people who loved me was priceless. The answer came, but again in His perfect timing.

At times, the sinking feeling of this period of my life was so great that I feared staying too long or getting stuck. It was, at times, easy to view myself as weak and ill equipped to go through but was reminded consistently to remain in faith. That it would eventually be well and all of us involved would become accustomed to the new color and contrast the world had without Dad being a part of it.

So much more compassion comes up in me due to my experience with this, and my faith was increased as my heart mended. I knew God was with me and that I could count on true friends.

I mentioned the fact that I helped others out in similar situations; so much so, that I was asked to start up the bereavement ministry at our church to walk with others through their times of grief and letting go. It was the way that God used my pain for His purpose. The fact that you can be of assistance to others is remarkable when the experience is so personal and sometimes private. That's the way God works in the kingdom. He uses folks that may not have taken courses in the ways of ministry or whatever other endeavor you're to lead or be a part of. However, through the memory of your own time in that place, you can avail your aid by empathy, sympathy, and support for those who need your help. I was extremely blessed to know that I could help my friends and acquaintances in some way to cope and get through the initial days and times without their loved ones.

Ultimately, we, like Jesus, lift each other up, encourage

each other, and walk the good and bad times in our lives together so that no load is too much to bear. We are so much stronger as a team and even just knowing that others care a lot is so comforting. I'm most grateful for the way I grew closer to the Lord in that time of my life. His continued encouragement in prayer, and quiet time with Him and through others is often a reminder of His love. I still allow Him to fill the empty spaces.

If there is a wounded place in your heart that needs healing, an emptiness that needs filling, or a perplexing problem where you need His help, I know from experience that He's only a prayer away. "If you don't know what you're doing, pray to the Father. He loves to help. "You'll get His help and not be condescended to when you ask for it" (James 1:5-6, MSG).

"(What, what would have become of me) had I not believed that I would see The Lord's goodness in the land of the living! Wait and hope for and expect the Lord; be brave and of good courage and let your heart be stout and enduring. Yes, wait for and hope for and expect the Lord" (Psalm 27:13-14, AMPC).

# 3

# "Peter, What Did You Ask?"

I'm certain there were some perplexed, shocked, and amazed looks and inquiries on the other apostles' faces! Did they actually get a question to him before he took his leap of faith? Well, I imagine, when it was said and done, at least a couple, maybe all wished they had asked to walk on the water with Peter! He said, "And Peter answered Him, 'Lord, if it is You, command me to come to You on the water'" (Matthew 14:28). Extra boldness that Peter had. He had such drive and passion and eagerness. A true zealot. If we look at the way Peter asked, he said, "command me," recognizing again, the person of God Jesus was, but also the power behind the Words that came out of Jesus' mouth. He knew of all the historical accounts of miraculous happenings in the Old Testament from studies with both the Lord and whatever else he received growing up. He had witnessed much at Jesus' side also. He saw the posture of boldness that marked the miraculous at Jesus' commands. Blind received sight, demons were cast out, and lost were found. I believe that is why he asked Him specifically to "command" him to come. At the response Jesus gave, "Come!" Peter had no need to hesitate, faith propelled him. He didn't let his fearful flesh or hesitant doubt rule, but instead relied on the excellent record the Lord had in performing all He said and the power of His Words.

I think it's important to note that Peter didn't just jump out in childlike faith and excitement, without permission. Those of us who are parents can rely on our life experiences to direct our own children in or out of certain situations that are not safe. Whether they listen is their choice, and we've not only had to deal with the consequences of bad choices ourselves but have helped our own navigate fearful moments, injury recoveries, and the sad waves of time outs. Asking permission can be so underrated and ignored.

I believe the greatest influence Jesus has on me and many whom choose it is His example of living. When we see, hear, and absorb the tremendous love, kindness, and all other good character traits He displayed to the world of His time, and embody those traits to the best of our ability, we allow ourselves the opportunity to become the living epistles that can have great impact. Leaving room for His power to strengthen the weaker manners we have is vital to going farther than we can on our own. As it says in Philippians 4:13 (JUB), "I can do all things through Christ Who strengthens me."

So, where we have our greatest challenges and defects He can come in and teach us a new way of moving, speaking, handling, and being with those we relate to.

I and my husband have been extreme influences on our children. This is both a plus and a minus! Those of you who are parents might attest to the fact that a smile will come to your face when you see your child display the kind of good and wholesome behavior you teach through your own living as well as the way you guide them. Proverbs 22:6 (KJV)says, "Train up a child in the way he should go: And when he is old, he will not depart from it."

The opposite is also true for some of us. That is, the occasional grimace that accompanies the realization that you've seen a bad behavior come out of that precious offspring of yours that was also learned under your tutelage. Ouch! I look like that, too? Thank goodness there's no time limit to the maturation and improvement clock where we and God are concerned. Bit by bit, we as well as our children, are worked with, pruned, remodeled, and purified by our Father as He molds us into the persons, we are all meant to be. I'm so grateful to Him for His patience with me and my progress! Some habits are harder to shift than others—can I get an *amen*!

## A FRESH PERSPECTIVE

Peter knew that he was not immune to a bit of lowering to other depths from the top of the sea. He was, after all, a fisherman and knew the seas and their fierce storms as well as the ultimate peaceful smoothness. His respect for the might and unpredictability of the water kept him humbled before the Man who could shift all past experiences and create a new adventure that had never, at least to my knowledge, been accomplished before by anyone. I'm sure he also knew the certainty of sinking if he were to just walk out by his own power!

How absolutely refreshing to learn something new of the world you are so familiar with and with the one you've come to admire and respect so fully! Peter's water world of fishing was as routine and professional as any other person's occupation at that time. He was successful, as he stayed with fishing for a time after Jesus died.

## "PETER, WHAT DID YOU ASK?"

Charting a new path on top of the waves, are you kidding me? Just a few steps, that's all I'd need. That's all he took, although it's not precise exactly how far he went—but he went.

I can relate to the experience of life ventures with someone new. I was brought up in a family that loved to go on vacation (I have yet to meet one that doesn't). We traveled extensively in the US and had a few favorite spots that we frequented. The Jersey shore has received rave reviews and with very good reason! It's ba-utiful! Very family oriented, fun, availability of great food and boardwalk activities. I can remember soaking up the sun with my sisters (with only #4 Coppertone! Back then, who knew?), body surfing with Dad, and hanging out with Mom collecting shells or playing a great variety of card and board games. Simple pleasures and now warm fuzzies.

I had also traveled with friends and had a great time discovering some of the most fun and memorable places with them! I feel so privileged to have spent some of the greatest of vacation days with my loved ones and friends! It's nice to see the wondrous things in nature and our world with those you're comfortable with and care for you as you do for them.

## TRAVELING BUDDY

Well, when I met my husband some time ago, one of the things we found we had in common right away was traveling. Going out for coffee, seeing a show, dinner with friends, and getting on the road all appealed greatly to us. He is my traveling buddy! We have similar taste in food — we'll eat most anything! There's an ease we have on the road, as long as I don't react to his driving, and he doesn't critique mine! We're so excited about reaching our destination, but the journey is so very pleasant also! We talk and talk and talk... and then, can be perfectly quiet in each other's company. Shopping, tours, historical landmarks, recreational activities, relaxing, eating different foods are common vacation occupations. If there's water, we're in it or by it, picture taking, followed by more relaxing and laughter! Our children, being brought up on the go with us, like it and have expectations of it as part of their lives. It's very rich and exciting and, most importantly, a wonderful time to share with our family!

There's a comfort, trust, and ease that goes with traveling with people who are our beloved. We know that the best is being decided upon for our benefit, and my husband keeps a tight watch on all his family! We are completely ourselves in the car and tent, hotel, timeshare, resort, or anywhere else we venture (that is, of course, unless we're in public places where we reign in our silly and somewhat loud volume to respect and not alarm those around us). We can't wait for our next time away!

I suppose, since Peter had walked so closely with the Lord for so long, there existed that same ease and trust wherever they went and whatever they did. It was another amazing and miraculous thing that the Lord was doing then, and it was being etched into their memories. In many things, I don't mind being a sideline audience member or spectator, especially when the dangerous and seemingly impossible is being attempted. In the moment though, Peter was very eager to step out of the boat and run to Jesus. I like to think that I would have done the very same thing, but when I remember all the times that I wasn't so eager to do what He was asking right away, due to procrastination, lack of confidence, or some other reason, maybe I might have been as the other disciples and watched instead. I, therefore, admire Peter for going for it! I'll have to keep my mind wrapped around this one to help. "When you pass through the waters, I will be with you, and through the rivers, they will not overwhelm you. When you walk through the fire, you will not be burned or scorched, nor will the flame kindle upon you" (Isaiah 43:2, AMPC).

## GETTING PERMISSION

As I write this book, I am waiting for my other book to be published. You see, like Peter, I'm not stepping out on my own without a heads up or "Go!" from God! I have flown by the seat of my pants entirely too many times to count. Sometimes the spontaneity of the task or activity worked out great! Other times, however, a pause, waiting on a confirmation or certainty of the next move I should make, has proven more prudent. After making the decision of my new venture, job, or sometimes not moving at all, noticeable peace is the most reassuring sign for me. I don't know about you, but I still haven't grown out of my childish ways when it comes to that bubbly excitement on the inside that comes at the discovery of something new and wonderful which I am about to embark on, a vacation my family or my sweetheart and I are about to take, a visit to see loved ones, dinner with favorite people, sitting down to write a new chapter, and to see where the uncharted journey will take me. I can get so pumped up about it that it's hard for me to sit and focus or collect myself enough to organize a plan too soon. I need to explode with joy and energy some way to release the kinetic sensation going on inside me!

When I was a small child, if my mother told me to

## "PETER, WHAT DID YOU ASK?"

be still once, she said it hundreds of times. "Be still" and "Child of grace" are the two most frequently used phrases I recall Mom using. Sometimes coming at a peaceful interlude, and other times through her gritted teeth when me or my other precious four sisters, or yes, me alone, weren't appearing quite as adorable as usual. I don't know if I might have been diagnosed with one of the many things, they label children with (I know I leaned toward the hyperactive end of the scale), but I'm sure glad I was told over and over that I was a child of grace! Now I understand the implications it had on my soul and my future. I don't know about you, but looking back on some of the crazy antics I did, I certainly needed the grace which my mom spoke over my character and life!

One simple example was an adventure I was having with my cousin, Penny, and my friend, Vinny, as we traveled cross country for me and Vinny to begin a new chapter of our lives in sunny California (me in the city by the bay, and Vinny in LA). Well, we were at the Grand Canyon and, needless to say, in awe at the surreal and absolutely gorgeous views to be had from wherever you looked! We hadn't yet gone into the visitor's center, and there were no signs or informational park plaques or kiosks to give us a word about what we were experiencing where we had decided to park. We wanted to walk, so I suggested a small path just beyond the guardrail (Okay, did they stop the zany one before they followed to a place of danger? No!). They didn't see anything wrong with it, so I led (the blind) my friends down this rock and dirt path toward the edge of the canyon. What? Mind you, we had no idea how far up we were, but considering it was the Grand Canyon, we were way up there.

After a little while, Penny had noticed that we were farther from the road and guardrail, and the path was thinner and too close to the edge. She decided to start back up (the smart and wise one) and followed Vinny as I went up a bit farther ahead. Well, outside of a few rocks flung at my cousin's cute head inadvertently by my friend, we made it to the road. Before I began my way up, I noticed a man and woman across the canyon from us. He had a camera and started taking pictures of us. "Weirdo," I believe, was the word I used to describe him. Well, by the time I had finished climbing back up, the couple had reached us, not just a few minutes later. The man, we found out was a nice person, asked if we were professional climbers. We laughed and told him we had just found the trail we were on and decided to risk it. He then asked if we were crazy! He told Penny and Vinny that if they had slipped and fallen, they would have been stopped by a good size ledge that seemed to jut out where they were, but if I had (look of dismay!) I would have, after tapping a small, outcropped stone, plummeted to my death! He said, I'm not some kind of weirdo (ha-ha!), but I have a picture that I don't think you should miss seeing! Well, he sent it to me, and I did look professional or insane and what a shot!

A bit later we did go to see what the visitor's center had to offer and also started noticing all these yellow signs of danger with a man falling with rocks falling with him. Well, I guess we didn't really have permission to go where no others go, but I am a "child of grace" and proved it then! He really is with us in times of trouble and lack of permission (sometimes inspired by our stupidity). "When they call on Me, I will answer; I will be with them in trouble. I will rescue and honor them" (Psalm 91:15).

## ABRAHAM'S OBEDIENCE

Abraham was a most obedient man. Those familiar with his story know of the most astonishing example when he took his promised son and seed to Mt. Moriah to offer him as a sacrifice to the Lord after being told to do so by God. I know that my God would need to be most convincing for me to even begin a journey with that kind of task attached to the end of it. Imagine this man, having left his father and homeland, growing old in a country that was not where he may have thought he'd inherit his land. Being told by God to go,

> "Get out of your country, from your family and from your father's house, to a land that I will show you.[1] I will make you a great nation; I will bless you and make your name great; and you shall be a blessing. I will bless those who bless you, and I will curse those who curse you; and in you all the families of the earth shall be blessed."
>
> **Genesis 12:1-3 (NKJV)**

Sounds good to me, too! Such a promise! I don't blame him for packing up his tent, family, and belongings and hitting the trail!

Things for Abraham and Sarah at that time went well, except for a couple kings who wanted Sarah for themselves, and a couple little stories (partial lies) on Abraham's part about his wife being just his sister. Outside of those things, as far as we are aware, they prospered and found their home lovely.

A bit further into the story of Abraham and Sarah, the Lord reminds Abraham about his seeds,

> "Look now toward heaven, and count the stars if you're able to number them," And He said to him, "So shall your descendants be."

## "PETER, WHAT DID YOU ASK?"

"And he believed in the Lord, and it was accounted to him for righteousness."

**Genesis 15:5-6 (NKJV)**

Well, God certainly has a way of reminding and bringing things into perspective and driving points home.

Let me remind you what happens next: Sarah gets impatient, disbelieves, or maybe thinks too much about her and her husband's ages, senior citizens, her barren womb, and devises her own method for those numerous stars to start representing descendants. She gives her husband her handmaid to birth them a son to start this super large family that they believed God for.

What happened to Sarah? Did she think God incapable? Wanted to have a part in it but lacked Abraham's faith, to the extent he had it for waiting on God? Pridefully thought she knew what God was up to? Well, she did, without being asked, something that would not have happened in my home! I would not give my maid to my man, no! Not happening! Even if it was not an uncommon practice in their time.

Long story short, God reminded Abraham a third time when He established His covenant with him (Genesis 17:9-10). He changed his name from Abram to Abraham (father of many nations). I believe at least in part to differentiate between the man who did not, "Walk before Him blameless and the one who did" (Genesis 17:1). As Abraham, he was first immediately obedient to the Lord when he circumcised all the male babies eight days and older up to and including himself at ninety-nine years old. This account is found from Genesis 17:10-14, and 17:22-27. I don't think details about it are necessary; however, it was a sign of the covenant God made with Abraham and all his descendants after him (Genesis 17:10-11, NKJV).

I mention it because of Abraham's quick response. Seems like a quick response kind of guy. Left his family at the Lord's urging, took his wife's handmaid at his wife's urging, circumcised the males in his charge from the Lord's urging, and eventually we know, he went to Mt. Moriah to sacrifice his son Isaac (which God stepped in and graciously prevented). Chapter 22 of Genesis tells this story, which ended with Abraham holding a knife over his child only to be prevented from harming him by an angel of the Lord saying, "Do not lay your hand on the lad, or do anything to him; for now, I know that you fear God, since you have not withheld your son, your only son from Me" (Genesis 22:12, NKJV).

Abraham received some tough requests from the Lord

and was ready to do whatever He said when He said it. It caused him to be blessed richly. He didn't live to see the billions of descendants promised him, but the promise came true and continues to. He was a man bent on serving his God and believing He had his best interest in mind when he did what he was told. He believed God knew what He was doing. His own son Isaac inquired of him,

> "My father!" And he said, "Here I am, my son." Then he said, "Look, the fire and the wood, but where is the lamb for the burnt offering?" And Abraham said, "My son, God will provide for Himself the lamb for a burnt offering."
> 
> **Genesis 22:7-8 (NKJV)**

Yes, saying it like that instead of saying what God told him to do kept Isaac from running, since he didn't know the truth, but more importantly, it allowed faith and hope to rise in Abraham as well as the strength to endure the impossible task at his hands. For those of you who know the story, a ram happened to be stuck in a nearby bush, so God did indeed provide as Abraham said, and they sacrificed the ram that He provided. Such obedience is another great example for us to follow.

Many places in the Bible stress obedience as well as doing what God says and not sometimes what we interpret differently or just decide to do instead because of influences and council we might get from others. God is clear, not confusing or vague. He may not give us all the puzzle pieces we need at a given time to understand what it is we're going to do or achieve by the end of a task, but He is faithful. He gives us as much information as we need to take the next step, jump out of our own boat, and begin a new venture or continue the one we're on with Him, toward the next place He takes us. Is it time for you to jump in?

# 4

# *Take Courage!*

The last few verses, that deal with fear, that we'll look at are the initial ones of the text we've been studying, when Jesus is seen by the apostles walking on the water:

> "When the disciples saw Him walking on the lake, they were terrified. 'It's a ghost.' they said and cried out in fear."
>
> **Matthew 14:25 (NIV)**

> "It is a ghost! And they screamed out with fright."
>
> **Matthew 14:25 (AMP)**

> "And when the disciples saw Him walking on the sea, they were troubled, saying, 'It is a spirit;' and they cried out for fear."
>
> **Matthew 14:25 (KJV)**

Jesus didn't hesitate to alleviate their discomfort, "But Jesus immediately said to them; 'Take courage! It is I. Don't be afraid'" (Matthew 14:27).

Three short statements out of Jesus' mouth to combat the terror that had risen on them as they were sailing the rough waves and suddenly greeted by the sight of what they thought an apparition. He shows Himself to them in His calming and commanding voice. Giving them directions on what to do to obtain their peace again. So effective was both His advice and their obedience, that Peter, as we've already discussed in this book, wanted to hop out the ship and run on the very waves that had just troubled him! Enough of Peter's venture for now, let's focus on Jesus' urgings. "Take courage" (Matthew 14:27).

Courage is the commodity that the Lord recommended that the apostles pick or chose instead of the one they were currently amid holding onto, which were terror and fear. Courage, according to W*ebster's* is a noun referring to the quality of being brave, valor. In Greek, *Talamo* means "to dare, have courage," to assume resolution to do a thing, to make up the mind, in this case, to be courageous. So yes, He was telling them to do it, and they needed to take the initiative to make it happen. In other words, just listening to Him say those words to them was not sufficient. That's why I believe the translation that says take courage, go possess it, apprehend it, own it, is the most profound in understanding more clearly what it was He was expecting of them. And, if they were holding onto courage, they would no longer be grappling with fear. It is certainly our choice to have the presence of mind to decide on faith instead of fear. To be brave in the face of frightening situations. In the Greek translation, it is a position of daring to be courageous as Peter decided to be with Jesus' calling.

## FIGHT FEAR WITH FAITH

While in the midst of addressing some of my own issues, I asked the Lord to help me understand what my greatest weakness was and where the enemy was most easily gaining access into my life and able to trouble me. He told me fear. Well, it wasn't surprising, as I was no stranger to the state of fear, appearance of being frightened, or experiencing general anxiety or extra concern where someone else would have none of it. So, what did I do to overcome it? I used the Word of God against fear and all the other attributes and characteristics associated with that challenging state of being. One of my favorites and memorized in the beginning of my attack on fear was Isaiah 41:10 (NIV), "So do not fear, for I am with you; do not be dismayed, for

I am your God. I will strengthen you and help you; I will uphold you with My righteous right hand."

So, again, these verses put forth a directive from God. He said, "do not fear." He says it again in Deuteronomy 31:6 (AMPC), "Be strong, courageous and firm; fear not nor be in terror before them, for it is the Lord your God Who goes with you; He will not fail you or forsake you."

Remember that we already saw a similar scripture in Joshua 1:5 in the chapter about sinking in fear. When God repeats Himself like this, saying "fear not," there's good reason and we need to be aware of its implications for us.

Psalm 91 is a most excellent help also with verses like:

> [1]He who dwells in the secret place of the Most High shall remain stable and fixed under the shadow of the Almighty (Whose power no foe can withstand) ...
>
> [3]For then He will deliver you from the snare of the fowler and from the deadly pestilence. [4]Then He'll cover you with His pinions, and under His wings shall you trust and find refuge; His truth and His faithfulness are a shield and buckler. [5]You shall not be afraid of the terror of the night, nor of the arrow (the evil plots and slanders of the wicked) that flies by day. [6]Nor of the pestilence that stalks in darkness, nor of the destruction and sudden death that surprise

and lay waste at noonday. ⁷A thousand will fall at your side, and ten thousand at your right hand, but it shall not come near you. ⁸Only a spectator shall you be (yourself inaccessible in the secret place of the Most High) as you witness the reward of the wicked. ⁹Because you have made the Lord your refuge, and the Most High your dwelling place, ¹⁰There shall no evil befall you, nor any plague or calamity come near your tent.

**Psalm 91:1, 3-10 (AMPC)**

The list goes on of descriptions of angels keeping watch and our love and faith in God causing Him to honor and deliver us. I wish to focus on some of the phrases that helped me most.

So, we are to dwell in the secret place of the Most High. It's a unique and personal place for each of us. Where is it? Well, for one, the Bible tells us that He inhabits our praise. "But You are holy, O You Who dwell in (the holy place where) the praises of Israel are offered" (Psalm 22:3, AMPC).

Although we don't have to be in a church service to offer Him a real and authentic praise, we can be in the privacy of our own homes and give Him glory in words and songs like David did and get His undivided attention. I sing to Him more now. There's a song by Pastor Clint

Brown called "Alone" sung from God's perspective and the lyrics are simple, telling us how He loves it when we praise Him by ourselves, alone:

> You don't need majestic choirs with awesome voices raised,
>
> you don't need a congregation to offer Me your praise,
>
> you don't need a mighty orchestra to bless me with your song, you get all of My attention,
>
> when you worship me alone.
>
> I love to hear you when you sing your song, and you worship Me, alone.
>
> (Clint Brown/PYPO Publishing)

If God also inspires beautiful music like this, it's true, He loves our private and personal praise. He's assured me it's so.

I also know that faith pleases Him and when we believe the best even when surrounded by the worst or great challenges, this can make Him happy. The Bible in the book of Hebrews 11:6 (AMPC) says, "But without faith it is impossible to please and be satisfactory to Him. For whoever would come near to God must (necessarily) believe that God exists and that He is the rewarder of those who earnestly and diligently seek Him (out)."

And in that same verse, it also says He rewards those who are seeking for Him to spend time, tell Him how wonderful He is, or to allow Him to be the one who consoles and councils us when we need it more from Him than any other source, because the response will be perfect.

So, He inhabits our praise and faith and seeking Him pleases Him. The list goes on, but that's sufficient to talk about the next part of Psalm 91 which describes the way He is around us when we're in His presence. Verse 1 says that when we get close to Him, we're so close, He shadows us, with what? Verse 3 says His wings or pinions, but their called "everlasting arms" in the Word also. "The eternal God is your refuge and dwelling place, and underneath are the everlasting arms..." (Deuteronomy 33:27, AMPC).

Okay, picture the strongest person you know with their arms around you. So good is the protection, it seems as though nothing can get in, and you are so safe, you'd rather not leave. Now, imagine those arms instead being God's, although invisible, they are far more powerful in ways we don't understand, and in this position, nothing can get in.

"Finally, be strong in the Lord and in His mighty power" (Ephesians 6:10, NIV). "In conclusion, be strong in the Lord (be empowered through your union with Him); draw your strength from Him (that strength which His boundless might provides)" (Ephesians 6:10, AMP).

We are limited in almost every way. He is limitless. All power and glory and honor and, and, and belong to Him. He's all we need and everything we need, when we need it. So, in this very protected and good place, we are kept from many things. A few are listed in Psalm 91 above: He delivers us from dangers (snares and traps; pestilence; sudden death), He shelters us so well, that we aren't afraid of terrors at night; arrows (evil plots and slanders) that go on by day. The Bible says we'll only be spectators (ourselves inaccessible in the secret place of the Most High) as we witness the reward of the wicked. Wow! Then it continues, because we make God our refuge and dwelling place, no evil will befall (come on) us, nor any plague or calamity come near our home.

> Because he has set his love upon Me, therefore will I deliver him; I will set him on high, because he knows *and* understands My name [has a personal knowledge of My mercy, love, and kindness—trusts and relies on Me, knowing I will never forsake him, no, never]. He shall call upon Me, and I will answer him; I will be with him in trouble, I will deliver him and honor him. With long life I will satisfy him and show him My salvation.
>
> **Psalm 91:14-16 (AMPC)**

## TAKE COURAGE!

Our love for Him will cause us to praise and glorify His name, and in return, when we call on Him, we receive His company in our troubles as well as answers to that call or prayer. He delivers us out of whatever trial, challenge, bondage, tough situation we might find ourselves in, and honors us too. I don't know about you, but at the end of my challenges and trials, I honestly don't feel that I deserve to be honored for the reason of those trials. Being fearful instead of faithful, angry instead of peaceful, sad instead of joyful when those things are at the root of the challenge (you can fill in this sentence farther with whatever was at the base of your weakness or fall). My own list can certainly be extended. He is just the type of God that looks beyond the challenge and gets to the heart of us. The true "us" of His creation. It's the turning to Him and relying on Him that puts us in the position of the child in need of His expert Fatherly character, that I believe He so wants us to get to. Sooner than the obstacle can cause any real extensive hurt or damage to us or anyone else. He wants to wrap those loving arms around us, yes for protection, but also to help us walk when we're too weak or cover our shame if we need that too.

Have you not known? Have you not heard? The everlasting God, The Lord, the Creator of the ends of the earth, does not faint or grow weary; there is no searching of His understanding. He gives power to the faint and weary, and to him who has no might He increases strength (causing it to multiply and making it to abound). Even youths shall faint and be weary, and (selected) young men shall feebly stumble and fall exhausted. But those who wait for The Lord (who expect, look for, and hope in Him) shall change and renew their strength and power; they shall lift their wings and mount up (close to God) as eagles (mount up to the sun); they shall run and not be weary, they shall walk and not faint or become tired.

**Isaiah 40:28-31 (AMPC)**

Now, I know some might be wondering how the Word can help? First, you read it. Then read it again and again and again until it gets in and is a part of your thought process. Next have faith to believe that The Word of God is true and yes, for you too! It was written a very long time ago but is a timeless book of love and promises and ways to live out these lives of ours with integrity. After faith takes root along with the particular verse of Scripture you need, your heart begins to change and then so does the rest of you.

I mentioned earlier in the book that sometimes answers to our prayers take time. Getting over a big problem in our lives can take a minute or two or weeks, months... You are worth the investment of your own time in yourself to help make that happen. Letting go of fear, or whatever your unique challenge is. Then trust that God will do the rest. Remember, your faith in His Word pleases Him and moves Him to action on your behalf.

Therefore, take heed and learn these power-filled Words of our Bible that are capable of salvation, redemption, healing, deliverance, peace, strength, joy... Also go explore and find more that suit you and comfort you, not only in the times of adversity, but also on the mountaintop with the Lord. Then believe you will receive the truth in your own life as it comes out of your mouth in faith, like in my case and the apostles on the boat, to remove fear and take courage.

# 5

# The Walk Back to the Boat

I'd like to spend some time on a portion of the text in Matthew 14 (NLT) that I wonder if very many people focus on. I haven't seen or heard much about Peter's walk back to the boat with the Lord. The verses it's contained in are as follows:

> [29]"Yes, come," Jesus said.
>
> "So, Peter went over the side of the boat and walked on the water toward Jesus.
>
> [30]But when he saw the strong wind and the waves, he was terrified and began to sink.
>
> "Save me Lord!" he shouted.
>
> [31]Jesus immediately reached out and grabbed him. "You have so little faith," Jesus said. "Why did you doubt me?"

[32]When they climbed back into the boat; the wind stopped.

I'm quite sure many of us had times in our lives that stand out because of the way Jesus walked with us on our way to or out of a situation we've been in. From an exciting and scary faith journey like Peter's or any other number of ventures we've been on that He's accompanied us and, in the end, saved us. I'm blessed to have heard many testimonies that confirm this.

As I reflect on the walk back, I remember a few preachers saying to get back to the place you began. Also asking, "What was the last thing He told you to do?"

In Peter's case He said, "Come," in response to Peter's request. In our case, during challenges, can we recall what it was that we were supposed to do next? Not that trials won't come as we are being obedient, Jesus told Peter to come to Him. Jesus knew the rough sea and waves were going to surround Peter. Jesus also knew He had dominion over the waves and water (and all else). It became a teaching moment for Peter and the apostles to trust and not lose faith in God.

Much emphasis is placed on Peter's stepping out in faith, as it should, because faith pleases God, as we've mentioned before in Hebrews 11:6 (the faith chapter). Now consider this verse in Ephesians 3:12 (AMPC), "In Whom, because of our faith in Him, we dare to have the boldness (courage and confidence) of free access (an unreserved approach to God with freedom and without fear)." Today, we may not be walking on the water with the Lord, but we can, without restraint, approach Him in prayer, praise, meditation, etc.

So, Peter stepped out in faith and went on this amazing journey. No one knows how far, a few steps, yards, I don't think it makes much difference at the end of the day, because, at the end, Peter was able to say that he walked on the water with our Jesus. I don't know about you, but that's one act I would like to have gotten in on. But the stepping out was only the beginning of the scene. After Jesus scooped him up, held him in those dependable and loving arms, then they walked back to the boat together! We cannot be sure how long or far the walk back was, as the only way to determine is by the Word. The word in this case is "When." "When they climbed back into the boat, the wind stopped" (Matthew 14:32, NLT).

Still walking on the water! Having a private conversation with the Lord on the waves. The only one in history that I know of that can claim this kind of time with Jesus.

Wow! What was said? Was Peter mindful enough to appreciate where He was and with Whom? But, as exciting as all that was, and in my eyes still is, the miraculous and lovely fact for me is the part where Jesus picks Peter up and helps him get back to the place he started, the place where he with such excitement and enthusiasm jumped out of the boat in the first place. He had the compassion and love for Peter to not leave him stranded, even though Peter's faith wavered, and we mentioned previously, that it's our faith that pleases Him. Instead, in His endless devotion to us and loving kindness, God helped Peter out of a dangerous situation and took care to bring him back to safety. I'd like to remind you of a couple things, first, Jesus has promised to never leave us nor forsake us, "For He [God] Himself has said, 'I will not in any way fail you nor give you up nor leave you without support. [I will] not, [I will] not, [I will] not in any degree leave you helpless nor forsake nor let [you] down (relax My hold on you)! [Assuredly not!]'" (Joshua 1:5, AMPC).

What did Peter give attention to? The waves, the adversity, the potential danger at hand? What do we choose to look at? It's hard to deny a tornado, tsunami, or other disaster heading toward you. You barely acknowledge it and then run to seek adequate shelter for the manner of peril headed your way.

## THE WALK BACK TO THE BOAT

It's a new way of life for some who chose to wear a mask in wisdom as we realize that many of our saved loved ones have died due to COVID, flu, etc.—even though we pray. When you're down in the dumps, lost your way, gone through a tough trial, or what may seem even worse than these in your eyes, He's there.

"Where could I go from Your Spirit? Or where could I run and hide from Your face? If I go up to heaven, You're there! If I go down to the realm of the dead, You're there, too! If I fly with wings into the shining dawn, You're there! If I fly into the radiant sunset, You're there waiting! Wherever I go Your hand will guide me; Your strength will empower me" (Psalm 139:7-10, TPT).

David, who wrote this Psalm, had gone through some amazing ordeals and fearful episodes in his life and yet knew the One that was there for him in his desperate times of need. I appreciate the transparency which describes his realization of God's omnipresent location in his life in this Psalm, and I understand what he means. At my own times of greatest need and challenge, when all others seemed scarce even to the point of betrayal, that same wonderful God was there for me. I honestly don't have to speak about any of my own trials as I'm sure just the mention of that word, trial, brings to remembrance your own moments of great need. If it feels right, maybe pause to gratefully reflect on how it went or how He was there.

Don't we all need a friend like Jesus? Someone to stick with us through thick or thin, Someone Who loves unconditionally, Someone to make a way where there seems to be no way. For me the only answer is yes.

Let's consider what really happened at the moment of Peter's weakness. He took his eyes off Jesus, need I say more? I pray you look deeper at the revelation here. When we step out in faith, the obvious next steps are to remain in faith, right? Well, like Peter, we fall out of faith, or perhaps forget that we have it! We rather focus on our challenges instead of the One Who gave us permission to move out in that faith and purpose in the first place. I won't linger here, as so many have put our strong and scared Peter through much judgement for his lack of correct vision.

I hope that we might instead see the more than obvious example of salvation contained in this short and poignant interlude between Jesus and Peter. Yes, Jesus made light of it when He said, "How little faith you have! Why did you doubt?" (Matthew 14:31, GNBDK). "'You have so little faith,' Jesus said. 'Why did you doubt Me?'" (Matthew 14:31, NLT). But just prior to this, Peter in desperation cries out, "'Save me Lord!'" (Matthew 14:30, NLT).

## THE WALK BACK TO THE BOAT

Yes, technically he wanted rescue from the waves, and some of our life's challenges are very obvious and, in our face, and minds as hindrances and harmful to our health and well-being. There is nothing more harmful, however, than our lack of faith in the One Who saves. Don't we as Christians all think we're walking in faith until adversity strikes and the position we've been in becomes compromised and the outcome of our daily activities and tasks shift from exciting and exhilarating to frightening and dangerous (in Peter's instance)? Or the way, mine and yours is individually: perhaps slow, frustrating, seemingly impossible, heavy, or without much hope? Where did we think Jesus went? Where did Peter think He went? Or perhaps we think He's not in it anymore or farther away, or we're being tested, maybe we didn't hear Him correctly, etc. Or perhaps we didn't stop to ask Him anything at all, went on our own strength or ideas. I ask you now what Jesus asked Peter, "Why did (do) you doubt Me?" Oh, all of us of little faith! Please know, I don't stand assuming that many of you take on these doubts I've mentioned, as I know some of you are steadfast and unmovable in your faith. I admire that quality so much and strive to make it more my own as I continue my life. I have hope as my anchor. Perhaps we can scripturally answer these and a few more questions for insight and understanding. Where do we think God goes or why when He's an omnipresent God for believers, do we doubt His place with us wherever life has taken us, both on the path He laid out, or the one we choose? The Bible relates this, "Because I, your God, have a firm grip on you and I'm not letting go. I'm telling you, 'Don't panic. I'm right here to help you'" (Isaiah 41:13, MSG).

If He has a firm grip, He's there with us even in our darkest and hardest times. He's the reason we are able to endure. He's walking through it with us and taking us either back to a safer place (the boat) or onto further adventures and higher heights away from what was problematic in us or around us. "Though a sinner does evil a hundred times and his life (seemingly) is prolonged (in spite of his wickedness), still I know that it will be well with those who (reverently) fear God, who fear and worship Him openly (realizing His omnipresence and His power)" (Ecclesiastes 8:12, AMP). "Surely His salvation is near to those who [reverently] fear Him [and obey Him with submissive wonder], That glory [the manifest presence of God] may dwell in our land" (Psalm 85:9, AMP).

Of course, these verses speak directly of our spiritual salvation which is so vital to be secured here while we still have the time. And reflects on our Father's involvement in all of it. Having such a very present and involved parent is blessing indeed.

## THE WALK BACK TO THE BOAT

When does God stop being God? When things go wrong? When people behave wrongfully toward us? When we behave wrongfully to others? Does He somehow forget how to be God for and to us? The Bible says in the book of Malachi 3:6, "I am the Lord, and I do not change" (NLT). "I am God—yes, I AM. I haven't changed" (MSG).

I do believe it is far easier to believe in our God in the more "regular" and "uneventful" moments. However, when we're the ones that lost the loved one, endured the storm or fire, pandemic, be they literal as we're witnessing daily in the news around the world, or inside, the silent storm within us, these challenge our faith as well as our peace, hope, and joy. I know it's hard to be able to see God in it immediately, especially if, unlike Peter, He's not visibly right in front of our face and the obvious answer to our prayer and cry for help. I believe we can acknowledge later, if not right away, how He was involved in the times we perceive Him scarce or aloof maybe unrecognizable to us as we look instead at the trauma or circumstance so apparent, close, and real. That is exactly where faith can grow, "The fundamental fact of existence is that this trust in God, this faith, is the firm foundation under everything that makes life worth living. It's our handle on what we can't see" (Hebrews 11:1, MSG).

PETER'S FRIEND JESUS

## SPEAKING TO HIM AND ABOUT HIM

As a woman of faith and strong belief in the living person of God my Father, His Son Jesus my Savior, and the precious Holy Spirit, I lean on the remembrance of the times in my past that He brought me through times of trial and hardship. Sickness in my childhood or that of a loved one that turned into healing and wholeness with the removal of pain and weakness; the renewed life after divorce or trauma that comes with the encouragement and hope in the Word of God spoken in a service or a friend's gentle touch or that whisper from the still small voice of God that is just what I need to hear. Since I have faith to believe what the Bible says is true, therefore what He said is true. I have many promises available to read, remember and put faith in, when my own faith seems to be inadequate or diminished and not sufficient for the path, I currently find myself traveling. It has been my experience that, as I speak certain verses and even whole chapters and books of the Bible and repeat them and hear the Words spoken gradually more faithfully and hopefully out of my own mouth, those Words of faith begin to come alive in my life.

"The Word is right here and now—as near as the tongue in your mouth, as near as the heart in your chest.

## THE WALK BACK TO THE BOAT

Just do it!" (Deuteronomy 30:14, MSG).

It's the Word of faith that welcomes God to go to work and set things right for us. This is the core of our preaching. Say the welcoming Word to God—"Jesus is my Master"—embracing body and soul, God's work of doing in us what He did in raising Jesus from the dead. That's it. You're not doing anything; you're simply calling out to God, trusting Him to do it for you. That's salvation. With your whole being you embrace God setting things right, and then you say right out loud: "God has set everything right between Him and me!" (Romans 10:8-10, MSG).

That is simply it. Putting Words of truth and rightness out of our mouth, hearing it over and over ourselves with our own ears and giving those Words a chance to be rooted deep in us, as deep as our hearts. Things like, "I am a child of God," "I am saved by grace," and "I can do all things through Christ which strengthens me!" The list of promises and qualities we take on by being in fellowship with God, saved by Him, are too numerous to mention, but very worth an investment of our time to investigate for ourselves.

Another way I've been very encouraged by the Word is through making declarations of it. I first began using inspirational books by pastors I very much admire and then that still small voice suggested I do my own. Therefore, I began listing the most poignant verses for my current situation and phase in life and decreed out loud during walks in my house the truths that I needed to hear the most.

Here's a short example that you can perhaps glean from:

> "Behold, I am the Lord, The God of all flesh: is there anything too hard for Me?"
>
> **Jeremiah 32:27 (AMPC)**

> "Ah Lord God! Behold, thou hast made the heavens and the earth by thy great power and stretched out arm, and there is nothing too hard for thee."
>
> **Jeremiah 32:17 (KJV)**

> "Do not be afraid or discouraged, for the Lord will personally go ahead of you; He will neither fail you nor abandon you."
>
> **Deuteronomy 31:8 (NLT)**

> "I declare I will 'Never be lazy, but work hard and serve the Lord enthusiastically.'"
>
> **Romans 12:11 (NLT)**

> "This book of the law shall not depart out of your mouth, but you shall meditate on it day and night,

that you may observe and do according to all that is written in it. For then you shall make your way prosperous, and then you shall deal wisely and have good success."

**Joshua 1:8 (AMPC)**

I have a variety of topics that I focus on, for example, my closer walk with the Lord and praising Him, my family's salvation, health and wellbeing for everyone I know, prayer for churches and the unsaved, safety, and many others. After my time confidently speaking these words over mine and my loved-one's lives, my countenance and inner self is refreshed and energized to complete my day, tasks, and other activities. It is worth taking some time to put your own collection together and putting into the atmosphere what the truth of the Word is for you (even if it doesn't look like it's happening in your life yet!), and when you get more confident about those declarations, start a new more relevant list.

## PETER'S STRENGTH

Yes, for a moment after incredible courage and delightful exuberance, Peter had a moment. Call it what you like, but that moment is what made the rest of his water walking so precious. Yes, here was big, brave, and bold Peter again

## PETER'S FRIEND JESUS

stepping forth in great force, and then quickly humbled by a trip up. What a privilege he had being scooped up and able to be corrected and told simply and plainly what was wrong, "Why did you doubt, oh you of little faith" by the One Who was going to tell it like it is. And then be able to walk the rest of the amazing journey in the arms of his Savior, Friend, Master, etc.

I believe Peter's humility and cry out was his greatest strength! The place of falling and realizing you need Jesus is the best. Not that we stay there of course, I mean fallen. Jesus did help Peter up as He does us. I'm just so emphatically grateful to this amazing God Who much rather helps and redirects and councils when we need it, just loves as any good parent and friend would. Taking the time Jesus knew Peter needed to settle down and get back to enjoying the final steps of their walk. I believe God so wants us to be able as He does, to move beyond the place of failure and hardship and get back to the beautiful and abundant life He gave us. Throw the sins, weaknesses, and things that weigh us down behind us as quickly as possible and get back on track. That is what I tend to believe God was also talking to Peter, that he'd trip up again, and Jesus would again support him. He told Peter about it like this after to their boat interlude, "Simon, Simon Satan has asked to sift each of you like wheat. But I have pleaded in prayer

## THE WALK BACK TO THE BOAT

for you, Simon, that your faith should not fail. So when you have repented and turned to me again, strengthen your brothers" (Luke 22:31-32, NLT).

We are all capable of helping people to celebrate in times of joy. Our four children have graduated high school, set off for university and careers, and we find it very easy to walk this amazing and pride-inducing time of their lives with them in much joy! The tough moments with them are far less important and striking than their accomplishments.

However, real bad news and times are the reason I believe I turn to Jesus for those walks back to my own boat. My need to hear His Word about my situation, that He still is there with me, as well as for me, and that I just need to get my eyes and mind refocused on Him and the plan He has laid out. Those times in quiet solitude and devotion have become priceless as I watch my private world shift with the growth of my children and the changes in my relationships, our cities, nation, and world. It seems there's never been a time when we haven't needed to support our neighbors in times of challenge both nearby and globally, more. And at the same time, learn to pray for those who seem to insist on being enemy to anyone against their agenda and ideology.

If you find yourself in a place of difficulty, lack, tough

time, or stagnant perhaps, whatever it is, there is Someone so exquisitely capable and ready to walk you away from and out of your current place of life. Only your hesitancy will prevent Him from stepping in and then stepping out with you. I recommend you try a bit of faith and ask for the help you need from the greatest Helper I've ever had the pleasure of loving and depending on, my Jesus. He is a Great God! "Jesus told them, 'This is the only work God wants from you: Believe in the One He has sent'" (John 6:29, NLT).

# 6

# The Power of Prayer

"And after He had dismissed the multitudes, He went up into the hills by Himself to pray. When it was evening, He was still there alone" (Matthew 14:23, AMPC).

So, Jesus had sent the disciples across to the other side without Him. He also dismissed the crowds. He then proceeded to find a quiet and solitary place to be alone to pray. We all know what came next, miraculously Jesus caught up to the disciples in the boat by walking on the water. So, why mention the fact that He prayed first and then did the supernatural feat?

We know Jesus was a man of prayer; it is mentioned numerous times in the gospels. He taught the disciples how to pray (Luke 11:2-4), the miraculous happened as He prayed when He was baptized (Luke 3:21-22, and when He prayed for Lazarus to come back from the dead (John 11:41-43), blessed five loaves and two fish when praying (Luke 9:16), and as we just mentioned previously, He prayed that Peter's faith should not fail (Luke 22:32).

The list is very extensive when we talk about how many times Jesus prays. He practiced what He taught, to be the example of the power and effects of prayer.

To say prayer is important, from my perspective, is an obvious conclusion from years of having prayed and then having those prayers answered. Simply a necessary part of my life. My prayers were not necessarily answered as I might have expected, however, the answer was right. I have taken example from Jesus, although it took me a long time to become as devoted to it as I am now. It's become more of a meaningful element of my daily activities and such a real and intimate relationship builder for my walk with my God.

I must admit that this chapter both seems daunting and humbles me. How do I talk about Jesus praying? We actually are not privy to those prayers mentioned where He goes alone, as they were His private time with His (our) Father. We are only told many times in different parts of the gospels that He went away to pray alone. Good idea. One of the examples that He left us that is priceless when applied in our own day to day routines.

## THE POWER OF PRAYER

There are two examples of His eloquent prayers in the Bible which I'd like to mention. In the Gospel of John, the entire seventeenth chapter is Jesus praying to the Father on behalf of those in His circle of disciples and companions and friends. There is a purposeful mention of we future believers also, "Neither for these alone do I pray [it is not for their sake only that I make this request], but also for all those who will ever come to believe in (trust in, cling to, rely on) Me through their word and teaching" (John 17:20, AMPC).

The fact that we who came to believe in Him are included is comforting to me. It's one of the most loving, compassionate, selfless, and insightful chapters in the Bible about the heart of Jesus and His truly deep love for us and determined dedication to His purpose in coming and His trust in our heavenly Father. Amazing. It makes me want to seek a much deeper relationship with them, Our Father and Jesus, due to the reflection of the love spoken about and toward us. A few of my favorites:

> "And now I am coming to You; I say these things while I am still in the world, so that My joy may be full and complete and perfect in them [that they may experience My delight fulfilled in them, that My enjoyment may be perfected in their own souls, that they may have My gladness within them, filling their hearts]."
>
> **John 17:13 (AMPC)**

I do understand what Jesus meant by wanting to share His gladness with us, only he went deeper, that His gladness would be "within us." And when that occurred, His joy would be full and complete, when we accepted the meaning behind the purpose He had coming down to earth—to save us. And He would be complete and full in joy when that happened. Notice He didn't answer that His joy might be complete when He accomplished what He set out to do, but rather, when those He did it for, took it to heart and accepted the fact that His purpose here was to do all that He did for us. I pray to emulate Him more in this way than any other, that I would be so selfless, that my needs would be the fulfillment of other's needs. In the "me" society we live in, there are so many opportunities to take care of us and be so occupied with those activities, that we're drawn away from seeing the needs of others around us. I know well that we also live in a society that cares deeply, because at the moment a tragedy happens, 9/11; hurricane Katrina; and now COVID-19; terror in our schools; wrongs against the innocent and righteous in our towns; many jump into prayer mode, help financially and other ways. I am more referring to the everyday reaching out to the ones who need the helping hand. The kind look, uplifting word, etc. I don't believe that role is designated for the Mother Teresa's, Popes, Bishop Jakes', Joel Osteen's, and Billy Graham's alone but rather for us all.

"I do not ask that You will take them out of the world, but that you will keep and protect them from the evil one."

**John 17:15**

"Sanctify them, [purify, consecrate, separate them for Yourself, make them holy] by Truth; Your Word is Truth."

**John 17:17**

"And so for their sake and on their behalf I sanctify (dedicate, consecrate) Myself, that they also may be sanctified (dedicated, consecrated, made holy) in the Truth."

**John 17:19**

"Father I desire that they also whom You have entrusted to Me [as Your gift to Me] may be with Me where I am, so that they may see My glory, which You have given Me [Your love gift to Me]; for You loved Me before the foundation of the world."

**John 17:24**

"I have made Your name known to them and revealed Your character and Your very Self, and I will continue to make You known, that the love which You have bestowed upon Me may be in them [felt in their hearts] and that I [Myself] may be in them."

**John 17:26 (AMPC)**

The entire chapter is so very uplifting because of its contents and inspiration for Jesus praying it is *"us."* He reminds the Father of the times He had with Him in heaven and before the world came into existence. He also lovingly asks our Father to protect us from the enemy of our souls; to sanctify us by the Word; include us in His heavenly kingdom; and that the love that our Father gave to Jesus may be in us also and that He, Jesus will reside in us, our hearts. How amazing and deeply affectionate He displays His love toward us in these verses! The fullness of His purpose shining through the requests He asks of our Father. That, not only we'd be saved to obtain our eternal reward of a heavenly home, we would also be dealt with in a most benevolent manner through the Father's protection and love. I am so grateful to Jesus for this prayer, love letter if you will, not only to our Father but also to us whom chose to receive the blessing and honor and promises laid out within it for His friends. What a great chapter to refer to when seeking a model for praying for family, friends, church family, and also those we hope eventually come to know Jesus as their Savior. The Word is a book full of prayer and petition to put forth as we need and are inspired to by the Holy Spirit. I know, however, that the impact of these Words of unconditional love from my Jesus are some of the most important and influential for the reassuring of my faith.

## SPEAK THE WORDS OF POWER

The other place of powerful prayer I've learned from is where Jesus, like mentioned already, was alone in prayer. Isn't it so reassuring to know that our Father God listens to our prayers even if we're praying by ourselves, solo, just us alone? I believe we have been given the lines,

> "And it came to pass in those days, that He went out into a mountain to pray, and continued all night in prayer to God."
>
> **Luke 6:12 (AMPC)**

> "But when you pray, go away by yourself, shut the door behind you, and pray to your Father in private. Then your father Who sees everything, will reward you."
>
> **Matthew 6:6 (NLT)**

> "Let them all join in with this orchestra of praise. For the name of The Lord is the only name we raise! His stunning splendor ascends higher than the heavens. He anoints His people with strength and authority,

showing His great favor to all His godly lovers"

**Psalm 148:13-14 (TPT)**

"He shall call upon Me, and I will answer him; I will be with Him in trouble..."

**Psalm 91:15 (KJV)**

So many good things come from our times of prayer with our God. The verses above promise: reward as God sees us pray, gives us strength and authority when our prayers of praise go up God answers us, and is with us in trouble. Wow! And that's just a few of the things promised from our time alone with God in prayer.

Getting rewarded for spending time with God seems unnecessary since the very time we are engaged in those precious private encounters brings peace, joy, and strength. To know that He goes beyond those moments in His presence to give us more than spiritual fulfillment and answer our physical, mental, and emotional needs as well, indicates that He is generous beyond what our finite minds can think or even sometimes believe. He knows our needs and wants to give the fulfillment of them. He is our Father. "The work they do will be successful, and their children will not meet with disaster. I will bless them and their descendants for all time to come. Even before they finish praying to me, I will answer their prayers" (Isaiah 65:23-24, GNTD).

We'll also remain stable and fixed, as mentioned earlier in Psalm 91:1. The definitions of these words show their profoundness when in our lives. In *Webster's* to be stable means to be firm in character, purpose, etc. steadfast; not likely to change, lasting. Fixed in the dictionary is defined as being firmly in place; established and settled; resolute; persistent. So, praying, time speaking to the Lord, will help us be more grounded and all the above in daily living.

I love the sound of those personality qualities very much and am encouraged to expect them as I do choose to go to Him often in prayer.

You see, I feel like a decent part of my life I was like a wave tossed by the sea, undecided, ambivalent, hesitant. I became stuck due in part to the dual perceptions people had of me. On one hand, sometimes I was told how smart, terrific, destined to succeed and make a good mark in the world I was as an individual. On the other hand, memories of harsh words and judgements against me, comparisons to others, and being rejected were all contributing factors to this place of bombardment and confusion between the two opposing forces of appraisal of my value and my worth within me.

"...For he that wavereth (in her faith) is like a wave of the sea driven with the wind and tossed. For let not that man think he shall receive any thing of The Lord. A double minded man is unstable in all his ways" (James 1:6b-8, KJV).

I knew I had some redeeming qualities; I just somehow couldn't convince myself for long enough to believe what I heard of my goodness, even in the Bible, until I began to spend more quality and precious time with my heavenly Father. I know the truth of the words, "Draw nigh to God, and He will draw nigh to you. Cleanse your hands, ye sinners; and purify your hearts, ye double minded" (James 4:8, KJV).

I know that for some, reading is believing, and many times it is for me also. I know that the truth of the Bible is in its entirety. I suppose there was some area on the inside that I felt just didn't measure up or make the grade to deserve all the promises and blessings God has for us. At this point however, I declare the Words of God in faith and if my faith isn't there, I speak and declare until my faith has risen to believe the truth of the Word.

"And you will know the truth, and the truth will set you free" (John 8:32, NLT).

# 7

# A Final Thought

Peter's friend Jesus proved to be an excellent example of a prayer warrior, rescuer when times got seemingly dangerous and uncomfortable, a trusted friend to tell him honestly where Peter stood on matters such as faith, anger, and so much more.

As I spend quality time conversing with the Lord and seek to be in His amazing company, I realize how much more complete and lovely my life is with Him in it. He has also rescued me, told me my strengths and gifts through the Word, as well as my failings and weaknesses. I have been instructed in prayer and walking out this life with purpose and courage by the same Jesus that walked with blessed Peter the Apostle on those waves so many years ago. The amount of gratitude I have can hardly be contained for the fact, first of all, that my God is alive, and secondly, ready, willing, and perfectly able to accompany me when I venture out of my boat, climb my mountains, rest in the meadows, and do whatever else has been or will be part of this wonderful life I've been given.

I encourage a deeper relationship with my Jesus so much that I can only say in the famous words of His mother Mary, "Whatever He says to you, do it" (John 2:5).

He's always calling us forward to the next step, stage, and plan in our journey. I hope that you consider, as so many have, to invite Him to be the most excellent traveling buddy you could ask for. And when you slip in doubt or unbelief, He'll be there to lift you out and walk with you back to the place you need to be.

*Bon Voyage*!

## MAKE A PLAN

So, how do I invite Him in? A simple heartfelt prayer is what it takes. I can help with that, and if you're ready you can say this one out loud:

"Jesus, I've heard about You and the way you are in other people's lives and the positive impact You've had on them. I'd like to give You a chance to be a friend to me also. Please forgive me for all I've done wrong. I also now forgive everyone who has wronged me. Please come into my heart, I make you my Lord and Savior. *Amen*."

## A FINAL THOUGHT

I am so delighted that you considered and prayed this prayer. As mentioned, as you seek Him, He will be found of you. Enjoy your walks with Him, wherever they go.

Blessings to you and those you love.

# 8

# Our Walk on Water

## the COVID-19 Encouragement

A step of faith is exactly what we're taking every day since this sickness began, and we became aware of it, in December 2019. A step of safety and security, a step of hope and belief in our fellow man, a step of trust in our government and all our front-line workers, and of course a step closer to a new unknown normal that our society will come to embrace.

For everyone's safety, we follow the recommended guidelines. We wear masks, wash hands and sanitize them every time we go anywhere or touch anything, keep our distance and stay home if we aren't feeling well. Common sense health tips in a very seriously CDC promoted way. We consider our own health and wellbeing, and in turn, affect our neighbors and all others we venture near to as we travel outside our cocoons. We keep in mind that other's cocoons aren't like ours and we consider them. We pray for a blessing on people's hearts who unexpectedly have had to say good-bye to family or friends that lost their battle against this worldwide common foe. We celebrate and appreciate all positive outcomes and recoveries and rejoice when we have made it another day ourselves.

For the ones who have lost a job, I pray your assurance in the God Who knows your name, your needs and knows already where the next opportunity awaits, I believe with you for it.

For those who have lost loved ones or are heavy with concern about the health of those close, I pray the peace that passes understanding come on you and yours as you courageously oppose a foe, we never picked a fight with.

If you are okay and have not been very inconvenienced or tried by this pandemic, please pray for people who aren't okay as you praise the God of us all for your situation.

I pray the continued strength, fortitude, health, and endurance of everyone considered front-line workers of all kinds. "May God bless you and protect you. May the Lord smile on you and be gracious to you. May the Lord show you His favor and give you, His peace" (Numbers 6:24-26, NLT).

I pray now that we will indeed come out of this challenge, "One nation under God, with liberty and justice for all."

I add the following scripture verses to comfort and help those who need:

> "So that He sets on High those who are lowly, and those who mourn He lifts to safety."
>
> **Job 5:11 (AMPC)**

> "God blesses those who mourn, for they will be comforted."
>
> **Matthew 5:4 (NLT)**

These bless me now as my family had to say goodbye to a precious Aunt who died in a nursing home due to COVID, as well as a dear Brother-in-law. Somehow, sadder for the suddenness, but joy filled because of their faith.

"No weapon that is fashioned against you shall succeed" (Isaiah 54:17a, ESV). This is the scripture the Lord gave me and my mother when she found out she had COVID. I am blessed to say, though her struggle was real, COVID lost the battle and Mom is completely recovered.

"'This (peace, righteousness, security, and triumph over opposition) is the heritage of the servants of the Lord, And this is their vindication from Me,' says the Lord" (Isaiah 54:17b, AMP). "And the prayer of faith will restore the one who is sick" (James 5:15, AMP).

Referring to the Word:

> "Don't lose sight of them. Let them penetrate deep into your heart, for they bring life to those that find them, and healing to their whole body."
>
> **Proverbs 4:21-22 (NLT)**

> And do not forget any of His benefits. Who forgives all your sins, Who heals all your diseases; Who redeems your life from the pit, Who crowns you (lavishly) with lovingkindness and tender mercy; Who satisfies your years with good things, So that your youth is renewed like the (soaring eagle).
>
> **Psalm 103:2b-5 (AMP)**

> "Beloved, I pray that in every way you may succeed and prosper and be in good health (physically) just as (I know) your soul prospers (spiritually)."
>
> **3 John 1:2 (AMP)**

CPSIA information can be obtained
at www.ICGtesting.com
Printed in the USA
LVHW080909070722
722894LV00012B/307